Real Estate Brands Ltd
PO BOX 2699
Springfield, OH 45501

*For more information about Real Estate Brands Ltd please
telephone 844.806.6577.*

Thank You!

Thank you to everyone at ROOST Real Estate Co.
that made our success possible and Andy Hayes
of Hucklebuck Design Studio for his creativity
and for the design of this book.

A REAL ESTATE AGENT'S GUIDE TO THE GOOD LIFE

WHAT YOU SHOULD EXPECT FROM YOUR BROKERAGE

By Chris McAllister

Founder / President / Real Estate Brands Ltd.

TABLE OF CONTENTS

Dear Real Estate Professional,

ROOST Real Estate Co. is the real estate company I have always wanted to work at.

ROOST is the product of my experience as an agent, broker, owner, trainer, and team leader. ROOST is about building and maintaining relationships, continuously adding value, and earning the referrals that give us the opportunity to do it all over again with new clients.

There is nothing more gratifying than helping somebody make a move they have been preparing their entire lives to make. ROOST is not for everyone, but for a select group of agents who want to be heroes to their clients, day in and day out, the job satisfaction and the potential income are unlimited.

Thank you for taking the time to learn about our business. Regardless of where your career takes you I wish you The Good Life.

Regards,

Chris McAllister

Chris McAllister
Founder
ROOST Real Estate Co.

INTRODUCTION

A DIFFERENT KIND OF BROKERAGE

We are not your typical broker. That's a great thing!

Most brokerages have two lines of business. They work with buyers and they work with sellers. At Real Estate Brands Ltd, we work with buyers and sellers too, but we also work with investors, and the people who rent from them.

We embrace 100% of the people who need a home, not just the 60% to 65% of the people who own real estate. This creates a very different kind of Real Estate Company for our clients and for our agents.

We work closely with investors. We help investors find, evaluate, purchase, and manage investment property. By offering Property Management services to our investors, they are more comfortable buying more properties.

Some people who rent their homes do so for their entire lives. Others will rent only for a few years before buying a home of their own. We help our tenant clients become home owners.

Because we work in the property management business, we've built relationships with skilled tradespeople to help all of our listing clients prepare and maintain their properties for sale.

The Real Estate Brands family of companies are referral based. We believe the very best clients are recommended by our existing and past clients. Our referral based marketing system keeps our brands top of mind with everyone we work with.

Our tenants become buyers, and refer new tenants and buyers to us. Our investors become repeat buyers, referring new investors, buyers, and sellers to us. Our buyers and sellers refer their friends, family and co-workers - again and again.

We are the real estate company people turn to at every stage of their lives. We are there when our clients rent their first apartment, buy their first home, their first investment property, and their retirement villa on the beach.

REAL ESTATE BRANDS LTD.
Smart. Passionate. Supportive. Approachable.

Meeting people where they are today, and helping them get to where they want to be tomorrow.

OUR FAMILY OF BRANDS

A QUICK HISTORY

When we first launched ROOST Real Estate Co. in Springfield, Ohio in January 2014, people would ask me "How did you come up with the name ROOST?" I would jokingly reply that "Zillow was already taken" and to a huge degree that is true. Here is how it happened.

I had a pretty good idea of what a real estate company should look like. By 2013 had been in the business for almost 13 years. I had been an agent at a successful local firm in 2001 and 2002 and became a RE/MAX franchisee in 2003. After the downturn in 2008 I associated my team again with the same local firm, and in 2012 began researching new opportunities including other franchises.

It quickly became clear that none of the companies I met with were the right fit for me. People I trusted urged me to create my own company, but the last thing I wanted was just another local 'Mom and Pop' brokerage. If I was going to do it, I wanted to create a business that was both scalable and sustainable. In other words, I wanted to be able to grow the business and succeed regardless of the inevitable ups and downs of the industry.

In early 2013, I met Andy Hayes who has a local business called Hucklebuck Design. I had seen Andy's work around town and I really liked his artistic sensibility. Andy and I began a dialogue that spring, that resulted in a set of brand 'guidelines' that really reflected a company I could get excited about. The core values of a smart, passionate, supportive, and approachable company, and a clear understanding where a company like ours would fit in the industry, all fell into place. The colors and fonts quickly followed.

What we needed next was a name.

Now you might think that would be the easy part... It was not. Andy and I generated literally hundreds of names, and at one point I even conducted a naming contest online. Every name we liked, needed to be run through three filters. The first was a simple Google search to see if the name was already in use. The second was trying to figure out if the Ohio Division of Real Estate would allow us to license the name. The third was doing a trademark search to see if the name could be trademarked.

After weeks of deliberation we chose ROOST Real Estate Co. The selection was a result of a process of elimination. However, I soon got excited about the name. It accurately reflects our unique position in the industry and in my opinion is a lot more fun.

Fast forward to Spring of 2015 and I find out that we cannot trademark ROOST Real Estate Co. after all. I will spare you the details but suffice it to say if you can't get a trademark for your name, you cannot sell franchises. At this point we were up and running in Ohio and newly licensed in Florida - but that was no help from a legal perspective. I absolutely believed, and of course still do, that our company could be a national brand someday but it could not be called ROOST Real Estate Co. everywhere.

That is where the alternate naming strategy came from. While we have what are called 'prior rights' for the name ROOST Real Estate Co. in Ohio, meaning we will be operating here as ROOST for years to come, we have no legal protection for the name anywhere else.

I needed another name, and better yet, a couple of other names for the company. If you have ever eaten fast food in your life, you are probably familiar with the hamburger chains Rally's and Checker's. Rally's and Checker's are identical restaurants with essentially identical logos that operate under one name or the other, depending on the state they are located in. Hardee's and Carl's Jr. employ a similar strategy.

So in effect, fast food was the inspiration for LiveHere and Lucky Town. We have filed provisional trademark applications for both of these names and hope to have formal legal protection for at least one, if not both, very soon. I like both names a lot but am partial to Lucky Town. I think it works on a lot of levels and is just plain fun. We all need more fun.

THE 4 FREEDOMS FOR REAL ESTATE PROFESSIONALS

THE 4 FREEDOMS FOR REAL ESTATE PROFESSIONALS

The purpose of this book is to give prospective agents and broker partners an understanding of how great being a real estate professional *can* be. Let's face it - for many of us, it is not so great. Our company offers a pretty compelling alternative to the way most agents and brokers experience this business on a day to day basis.

I do not see the point of being in the real estate business at all, if it does not allow for a superior way of life. There is way too much risk, hard work and potential heartache involved. Let's face it, there are easier ways to make a living.

Dan Sullivan founder of the entrepreneurial coaching firm Strategic Coach (who I will write more about later) says that successful entrepreneurs enjoy four 'freedoms'. The freedom of *time, money, relationship, purpose*. What might these four freedoms look like for a real estate agent?

Freedom of Time

The freedom of **time** means you are in control of your day. We've all heard becoming a Realtor® would allow us to work when and how we want. But at the end of the day, how many of us have control over our time? Whether we feel financial pressure to be on duty all of the time, or we lack the team and support to allow us to focus on what we know we should be doing – instead of what we feel obligated to do, our time is not always our own.

Freedom of Relationship

The freedom of **relationship** means choosing your clients. How many times has our confidence been depleted by working with people we flat out do not enjoy working with, because we have no other choice? Freedom of relationship means you work with, and work for, people that support and appreciate all you have to offer.

Freedom of Money

What about **money**? Yes, the real estate industry offers unlimited income potential. But let's be honest - if you lack the resources to claim your share of that income, real estate pays pretty poorly. ROOST Real Estate Co. is structured so our agents are achieving the highest overall compensation in the area, by making sure everyone focuses on what they do best – every day.

Freedom of Purpose

Which brings us to **purpose**. Why did you get into this business? Most of us want to help people make the big moves in their lives. We want to be heroes to our clients with every transaction. Our purpose is clear - to help people live the way they want to live, today. When your purpose aligns with your ability to help people, the money follows.

The 4 Freedoms
for Real Estate Professionals

Freedom from spending your **time** doing things you are not good at or that do not align with your goals. Freedom to do what you love and what you do best-make real estate dreams come true.

TIME

RELATIONSHIP

Freedom from taking on any customer with a pulse that happens to call your cell phone. Freedom to work only with clients and customers that respect you and value both you and your time.

Freedom from living closing to closing, and not having the resources needed to create stable income. Freedom to build a business that works for you by creating increasing value, leading to more referrals and increasing levels of income.

MONEY

PURPOSE

Freedom from continuously finding yourself involved in things you don't find meaningful. Freedom to work in a company with a culture that values your dreams and goals and is committed to seeing you succeed on your terms.

OUR WAY IN THE INDUSTRY

OUR WAY IN THE INDUSTRY

I see our company as a beacon of light in an increasingly dark and complex industry.

Yes, I said that out loud.

Let's face it, most of us are getting hit from all sides. Internet entrepreneurs skimming our listing information and using it to create leads they sell back to us, is just one example. Increasingly competitive, and often just plain mean, cooperative relationships with other agents and companies, is another. These are not bad people on the other side of the table. They are simply frustrated and scared, and sometimes it shows.

Buyers, sellers, tenants, and investors getting bad information from thousands of different media sources make our lives that much harder. And worst of all, potential buyers, sellers, tenants, and investors are starting to paint all of us in the business with the same brush. In many quarters of the market we are seen as interlopers and are held in contempt.

So how do we make our way in this world?

We make our way by becoming trusted partners and sources of good information and counsel. We do it by continuing to get better at what we do, by continuously expanding our capabilities as individuals and as a company. We are oriented toward growth and continuously adding increasing value. We work *hard* and we work *smart*. We also work by referral. And that allows us to work with people who already know and love us.

THE ESSENCE OF OUR ASPIRATION

THE ESSENCE OF OUR ASPIRATION YOUR BROKER AGE FOR LIFE

ABUNDANCE

ROOST REAL ESTATE CO

LUCKY TOWN

LIVE HERE

YOU
Smart
Passionate
Supportive
Approachable
Trusted Partners

THE GOOD LIFE

VS.

Chasing Transactions

SCARCITY

WORKING BY REFERRAL VS. CHASING THE NEXT TRANSACTION

Adding Value
Building Relationships
Being of Use
Collaboration
Predictable Income

Working By Referral

SURVIVAL

Fear
Waiting for Leads
Anxiety
Frustration
Living Closing to Closing

SELLERS THE INTERNET
INVESTORS
TENANTS
BUYERS
COOPERATING AGENTS

THE MARKET
Competition
Complexity
Unforgiving
Bad Information
All Agents are Alike

THE ESSENCE OF OUR ASPIRATION

Our core values of working by referral, creating an environment where our associates can do what they do best everyday, and working with buyers, sellers, investors, and the people who rent from them, set us apart from every other major real estate brand in the country.

We provide our Broker/Partners and our Agent/Associates with all of the latest and greatest technology and tools to enable them to build more and deeper relationships with their clients.

Our agents who have come to us from other offices, tell us this was the best move they ever made for their business. Not only did their sales improve but they were more profitable and had better control of their time.

In short, they increased their *freedom* and their *capabilities*.

When you come into one of our offices there is always something going on. People are excited, and that excitement is infectious. Many of our agents have home offices and do a lot of work in the field, but they look forward to being at the office.

Agents stop by just a few times a week and others make full use of their work space and the facilities. They are proud to meet clients at the office. And since there is always something going on, there is always someone on staff who can assist a client with the need to drop something off or sign a document.

Your Brokerage for Life

We expect to be the only brokerage you will ever need. Our goal is to grow, adapt, and create whatever new capabilities are necessary to support you, as our industry continues to change over time. We are alert to changes in the market and the ever-changing needs of our associates and clients. We will not be left behind. We will not allow you to be left behind.

We talk about our clients being able to rely on ROOST from the time they rent their first apartment, all the way until they buy their last retirement villa on the beach.

Our associates rely on ROOST from the day they earn their real estate license, through the days they hire their first assistant and assemble their first team, to the day they begin the process of selling their business and start looking forward to their own retirement villa on the beach.

Our agents can expect the support and coaching they *need*, at whatever stage they are in their career.

Why Working by Referral Matters

Working by referral is the essence of our business. Early on in my career I realized it was going to be much easier (and less stressful) to take the long view for my business and create advocates for my services and expertise. I soon realized this was a unique approach in the industry, because within two years my business rivaled those practicing 10 times as long as I had. And I still had room to grow.

From my earliest days in the business, I dreamed of creating an entire office—and later a company—devoted to building and deepening relationships with our biggest fans. Every new addition to my database was a deposit in my business *investment account*. Staying in touch after the transaction meant a steady stream of referrals and the opportunity to list the home I just sold at some point in the future.

I never had the dry spells that other agents had.

Of course being a *nice guy* and staying in touch is never enough. Creating fans for my business required acquiring more and more experiences and competencies that I could use to help council and guide my buyers and sellers.

In short, I had to continue to get better at what I did. More importantly, I had to learn to create more time to do more of the things I did well, and less of the things I could have someone else do. I have learned from experience there will always be people in the world I want to work with, and who want to work with me.

Working by referral allows me to approach our industry from the perspective of *abundance*. Abundance in this context means that I will continuously be able to add value, build relationships, be of use, and collaborate with my clients and business partners. At the end of the day, this creates a predictable, sustainable and increasing income for myself and my family.

The Alternative to Working by Referral is Unacceptable

As a new licensee I was told to go knock on doors, make cold calls, and walk the mall and pass out 10 business cards a day. Well, I could *not* do it. I did try. The fact was few people were home, landlines were already on their way out, do not call laws were on their way in, and the mall in my home town was already on the decline. (It is now up for auction as a foreclosed property.)

But now we have the internet.

The internet has, without a doubt, improved our world and our lives. It has helped make many agents (including myself) become far more productive than we ever dreamed possible. *It has also destroyed, and continues to destroy, the lives and careers of countless real estate professionals.*

Agents and brokers who relied on door knocking, cold calls and walking the mall, went out of business if they could not adapt to the world of Zillow, Realtor.com, Trulia and countless other internet based companies created to sell unqualified leads to real estate agents and brokers. Agents and brokers who used to chase leads and transactions door to door and at the mall, left the business when they could not figure out how to chase leads online.

What happened to the agents who used to walk the mall and figured out how to buy leads online? Many of them remain in the business, but exist in a hell they cannot escape. And sadly, the majority of agents who have entered the business since 2008, are experiencing this same hell.

I am sorry, but if you are an agent dependent on anything other than your personal book of business, database, referral sources, and your reputation as a professional who continuously strives to add value before and after a transaction is closed, you are toast. The idea of being told that I have to respond within five minutes to an unknown and unqualified inquiry that comes to me via the internet or I am going to lose that 'opportunity' fills me with anxiety and dread.

As I type this, I am freaking out. If you are waiting for your turn in a round-robin system for the next lead your broker deigns to graciously bestow upon you for your next check, you are in just as much trouble even if you don't have to pay a referral for the privilege. Chasing leads in an effort to create a transaction to make your next mortgage payment, is an existence that nobody deserves and nobody should ever sign up for.

Transaction Based Brokerages

Brokers and brokerages who work from transaction to transaction are perpetuating the public's view that all agents (and all brokers and brokerages) are alike. These transaction-based firms are helping to turn the art of helping people with the largest financial commitments of their lives, into a commodity. If all you have to sell is a commodity, you had better be the lowest cost provider in the industry. You need to be Wal-Mart—big enough and strong enough to set the lowest price and defend it at all costs.

Let's take this commodity or transaction based world view one step further. If the art of helping someone with one of the biggest decisions of their lives is just another transaction, what does that make the agent involved? In a transaction-based brokerage, are agents not interchangeable? Are not all agents alike? And if so, why invest anything at all into the relationship?

Most real estate firms today don't invest in their agents. The honest players in this group expect very little from their agents and invest accordingly. These 'body shops' provide the bare minimum services to agents at the lowest possible cost and still enjoy an acceptable return per agent. However, they need a lot of agents to make the model work.

These types of brokerages tend to have a lot of turnover but still enjoy financial success because they attract the greatest number of agents. It is a numbers game. If one of my 'honest' brokers has 100 agents and they charge each agent a base fee of $200 month for essentially holding their license, that is still $20,000 in income each month before any transaction or referral fees are collected. Some of these brokerages employ thousands of licensees and make millions of dollars a year.

The brokerages that make me crazy are those who are dishonest in their approach. These are what I call 'legacy' brokerages and brands that have been around for years and at one time were indeed leaders in the industry. As the business has changed, they have stayed the same, trading year over year on a diminishing reputation. These brokerages continue to charge their agents high fees in the form of a split, but do nothing to set themselves apart in a Wal-Mart world. In other words, they are charging 10X or more what the 'honest' brokerages charge their agents but offering nothing more in the way of service and support.

Working from transaction to transaction is what working from an attitude of *scarcity* looks like. People who are constantly chasing leads, working from transaction to transaction, stressing over when the next closing will take place, tend to believe that there is a finite amount of business to be had and that they had better fight, claw and scratch to get their share. I don't blame them for expressing their feelings of fear and anxiety when they are on the other side of the table from me. I would be scared to death also. I do however feel sorry for their clients.

The Real Estate Market of Today

It would be disingenuous of me to say there is never a place for a Zillow lead in the life of an agent. All agents, and new agents in particular, need to look at a lead as an opportunity to form a relationship and make an addition to their database. The contact is where the value is, and any resulting commission check is a bonus.

We pride our offices on being *Lead Generation Machines*. We enjoy referrals from past clients, people we meet through the internet including our own websites, open houses, current buyers and sellers, tenants and investors we manage for. The vast majority of the leads we generate are organic in nature -a direct result from working by referral - not from purchasing leads from the listing websites.

But let's face facts. Our agents and the general public are experiencing a real estate market that is increasingly competitive, complex, and unforgiving. The process is filled with bad information, frustrated participants on all sides, and an increasingly common world view that all agents are alike and can be traded one for another. Much of the public believes the most trustworthy sources of advice come from the internet or the program they watched last night on HGTV.

We Have an Alternative

The market of today is the perfect environment for ROOST Real Estate Co. and all of our agents and associates to thrive. A real estate professional that can bring order, a plan, a sense of control, and spirit of collaboration to the process of buying and selling real estate has a very bright future indeed.

Our unique ability, and the essence of our aspiration as an organization, is to continuously develop business opportunities and strategies that support and add value to the lives of real estate professionals and their clients. We brought ROOST into the world as the Smart, Passionate, Supportive, Approachable, Trusted Partner the industry needs today.

We train, develop, support, partner with, and equip the best real estate professionals in the business to work in, and bring clarity to, a market and an industry that sorely needs their expertise. We come to the market from an attitude of *abundance*. We add value, build relationships, do what we say we are going to do, and do it as well (or better) than anyone else. We confront fear and complexity in the market by working collaboratively with our clients and each other, and in return we enjoy ever increasing satisfaction and income.

The Essence of Our Aspiration

We will always be a company that aspires to greatness. The bar will always be raised. We aspire to be heroes to our clients on a daily basis. More often than not we succeed, but we are only human and sometimes we fall short. The difference is we always get back up, look for new ways to get better, and go back out and do it again. We aspire to be the best in a very tough industry. This is my life's work. We will never stand still. We want to be your broker of choice and always a cool place to work.

BE THE HERO

HERO

Adding Value

Being of Use

Trusted Collaborator

$

PASSION

Doing what you

love for people who

appreciate what

you have to offer

A SHOUT OUT TO DAN SULLIVAN AND THE STRATEGIC COACH

Ongoing education, and the continuous development of new personal and organizational capabilities, are the cornerstones of the Real Estate Brands Ltd culture. We pride ourselves on associating with the premier training and development organizations in the world, one of which is The Strategic Coach. (www.StrategicCoach.com)

I have been a client of the Strategic Coach since 2005. Strategic Coach was founded by Dan Sullivan and is the premier coaching group for successful entrepreneurs. To give credit where credit is due, much of my thinking about, and my ability to articulate what I think a real estate brokerage should be, is a direct result of my involvement with Dan's company and in particular my coach Adrienne Duffey. (Thank you Adrienne!)

One of Dan's core concepts is called **The Fundamental Relationship** (1). The Fundamental Relationship describes graphically how a successful entrepreneurial organization interacts with the world at large. The Fundamental Relationship directly inspired my thinking about **The Essence of Our Aspiration**.

The Essence of our Aspiration explains our mission as a company. Our mission is to create business opportunities and strategies that support and add value to the lives of real estate professionals and their clients. The real estate industry is complicated and dynamic. Our job is to bring a simplicity and sense of order to an increasingly chaotic and often punishing business.

WHAT SHOULD YOU EXPECT FROM YOUR BROKER?

First of all, you should expect a company, an office and a culture that is committed to supporting you so that you can support your clients.

You should expect to receive the tools, training, coaching, and support that will keep you focused on what you do best: generating leads, building relationships, earning referrals, closing transactions, and making dreams come true.

You should expect a broker committed to helping you build a business plan that will allow you to realize your personal and professional goals. A broker whose job it is to see you succeed on your own terms and by your own rules.

You should expect an administrative and support staff that share your commitment to your clients and are prepared to help you offer world class service every day.

You should expect the latest technology that supports our business, mission and values. You should find technology that supports your marketing and advertising initiatives, supports working by referral, and allows you to focus on what you do best.

WHAT WILL YOU FIND IN OUR OFFICES?

WHAT WILL YOU FIND IN OUR OFFICES?

Technology that supports our Marketing & Advertising Initiatives

We use the internet to not only advertise our listings but also to build brand awareness and to make an emotional connection with the public.

Each agent has a personalized ROOST landing page that puts them front and center as the brand. Our company website offers detailed information about our company and the services we provide.

We offer basic search functions on our websites through the local multiple listing service(s) as well. However, in an age when most homebuyers are going to Realtor.com for information, we provide enhanced exposure in the form of showcasing our listings and our agents.

A key feature of this service is keeping our sellers updated about how their properties are performing on the internet. All leads generated by our listings on Realtor.com go to the listing agent.

Social Media has become the number one tool for building brand awareness. ROOST Real Estate Co. has a dedicated marketing service building our presence and brand awareness through Facebook, Twitter, Instagram and YouTube.

Each agent receives a @ROOSTRealEstateCo.com email address to keep consistent branding.

Our marketing and advertising initiatives also have a place for print. We have partnered with **Holmes Printing** to create on-demand business cards, marketing brochures, postcards and various other mailers and collateral materials designed to build brand awareness and market share.

Technology that Supports Working by Referral

We close transactions – a lot of transactions – but it is the relationships we build along the way that keep our business growing and flourishing.

We offer each agent **Referral Maker** CRM (Client Relationship Manager). This desktop and mobile platform is offered by **Buffini and Company** our training and coaching partners. Referral Maker will allow you to track your referral creating activities, relationships, and transactions. Most importantly, it will help you turn these activities into an income stream that will support your personal and business goals now and well into the future.

A key tenant of 'working by referral' are the personalized Buffini and Company designed monthly Item of Value mailings. We will mail up to **100 Items of Value** each month to your very best clients - at no cost to you. This jump start to the Working by Referral business model is one of the most valuable services we provide.

Technology that allows us to do What We Do Best

A real estate professional focused on building relationships, generating leads, and closing transactions doesn't always have time for all of the 'backstage' activities that make the 'on stage' work possible. That is why we offer each agent a complete productivity package designed help eliminate activities that take time away from clients and customers.

Each agent is set up with an account at **Centralized Showing Services** or **Showingtime Showing Service** to eliminate the need to personally set up showings on their listings. Each of these services provide a mobile app allowing each agent to quickly and easily tailor the service to the needs of each seller. CSS automatically asks the showing agents for feedback and that feedback can be shared directly with the seller in real time.

Each agent is set up with a Dotloop account. **Dotloop** allows agents to create contracts and listing packages electronically on their desktop computers or mobile devices. It provides a secure platform for obtaining signatures electronically and ensuring that contract packages are complete for compliance purposes.

Each agent is set up with a personal **8X8** Phone Number. Our offices are equipped with an 8X8 state-of-the-art cloud based auto attendant and voicemail system. Through either a desktop computer or mobile app, agents direct their incoming calls to ring through to their desk, home office, cell phone, a fellow team member, or to voicemail, at select times of the day. Agents can be notified about voicemail messages via email.

The 8X8 system allows each agent to tailor their answering and communication services to the needs of their specific clients and market.

Making Sure It All Works

A key member of each office staff is the **Agent Business Manager (ABM)**. The Agent Business Manager's sole responsibility is to support the daily business activities of the agents assigned to him or her. The ABM manages all of the agent services discussed above and provides ongoing training and support as needed. The ABM's number one goal at ROOST Real Estate Co. is to ensure that our agents are getting the greatest benefit from the tools we provide.

WHAT SUCCESS WITH US LOOKS LIKE

WHAT SUCCESS WITH US LOOKS LIKE

Have an Ownership Attitude

When there is a problem, step up and take responsibility. Never report a problem without bringing a solution along for the ride.

Create Value

Continuously look for new ways to be of greater use to our clients and fellow team members. Look for new ways to contribute and help our clients realize their goals.

Take Initiative

Don't wait to ask permission to do the right thing when it comes to exceeding the expectations of a client. We expect you to do what is right.

Focus on Results

The road to ruin is paved with good intentions. At ROOST® we trade on performance, not promise.

Have Patience and Compassion

We serve a diverse client base with varied educational and socio-economic backgrounds. Not all of our clients will handle problems and conflict the way you or I might. Regardless, we will treat everyone we serve with the utmost dignity and respect.

Take a Partner

Some of our challenges are bigger than we are, or at least seem that way. Take a partner with another team member or team leader. Don't hide bad news thinking it will go away. If something feels wrong, it probably is.

Never Give Up

Mistakes and breakdowns in performance are learning opportunities in disguise. You will make mistakes – our hope is that you do all you can to never make the same mistake twice.

COMMON CONCERNS

THE COMMON CONCERNS

The two biggest concerns we hear from agents who want to join our brokerage are losing income during the transition, and the emotional turmoil involved with telling their current broker or manager that they are leaving. There is nothing harder than telling someone you are moving on— regardless of how good a business decision you know it is. Even if you are angry at or disappointed in the company you are leaving, the act of resigning causes anxiety for many of us.

I wish we had a solution for this, but we don't. We suggest writing a formal resignation letter and asking for a one-on-one meeting. There is no reason to get too deeply into the details at this point, as chances are your manager already senses something is amiss. Be the professional you are, but you owe it to yourself and your future to make a clean break and allow yourself to get excited about this new chapter in your life.

The second concern about losing income during the transition is valid. By some estimates agents can lose 20% of their income for the first couple of months at the new firm. At ROOST Real Estate Co., we attack this concern headlong with our **Quick Start Plan™**. Our brokers and Agent Business Managers begin to work with our new agents prior to actually making the move to ensure they hit the ground running. In our experience agents can expect an *increase* in business activity within days of joining.

THE QUICK START PLAN

THE QUICK START PLAN™

Hit the Ground Running

In a perfect world an experienced agent joining our company will have two weeks lead time before moving their license. This allows us to put everything in place that an agent needs to make a huge impact in the market, on day one. Of course sometimes things happen much faster and unexpectedly - and we adjust. As the saying goes however, those who fail to plan - plan to fail – and nobody wants to lose 20% of anything.

Checklist - Two Weeks Prior to Launch Week

☐ Order yard signs and name slats.

☐ Get picture taken at new desk for personalized website.

☐ Complete the 10 questions for your personalized website.

☐ Order personalized All About ROOST cards for welcome mailer.

☐ Create @ROOSTRealEstateCo.com forwarding email.

☐ Create .CSV or Excel file of database for welcome mailing.

☐ Obtain new office phone number and order new 8X8 phone.

☐ Create new Dotloop account.

Checklist - Week before Launch Week

☐ Finalize mailer for next Monday for release during launch week.

☐ Complete the personalized website build.

☐ Get new listing paperwork together in new Dotloop account.

☐ Set up Referral Maker and import .CSV file for first Item of Value mailing.

☐ Facebook post setup and 'boost' plan.

☐ New phone and desk set up.

☐ Business cards on hand.

Checklist - Launch Week

☐ Notify current broker of your move.

☐ Overnight paperwork or visit the Division of Real Estate in person.

☐ Release the personalized mailer to agent's database.

- [ ] Launch the website with agent's personal web address.

- [ ] Post 'Welcome Agent' and personalized website on Facebook and Twitter.

- [ ] Get new listing agreements signed with sellers.

- [ ] Place new signs in yards.

- [ ] Deliver new Board of Realtor and MLS paperwork

- [ ] Transfer Listings in MLS(s).

- [ ] Obtain Realtor.com and showing service logins.

Your Agent Business Manager and broker/manager will be instrumental in helping you make sure all of this – and more – happens during week one. As you can see, our goal is to ensure your transition is seamless and actually gives you an immediate income bump.

THE RHYTHM OF
OUR BUSINESS

THE RHYTHM OF OUR BUSINESS

I have already talked about the *Freedom of Time* that a real estate career can provide, from the perspective of spending your time doing what you do best. Now I want to talk about time in terms of free time and time off.

Getting control of your time is not easy. It requires intentional effort and more importantly an absolute self-confidence in the value you bring to the market. A real estate professional should not look at their practice any differently than any other professional. You would never pick up the phone and randomly call a doctor, lawyer, or accountant and demand an immediate audience.

Don't let anyone try to do that to you.

Having said that, there is a rhythm to our business. While working by referral undoubtedly makes for far more consistent income throughout the year, there is still a seasonality to the market. We need to be aware of it, and we need to make the seasonality work for us.

Having tracked my personal productivity, and the productivity of my agents, for several years now, I know exactly when I need to be 'in' my business, working 'on' my business, and when I need to be focusing on recovery and rejuvenation - so I can go out and do it all over again.

Holidays and Long Weekends

First of all, free time, time off, a holiday, or a vacation, should not be something you have to *earn* and reward yourself with. For a full time, 'all in' professional, regular time off is absolutely necessary to continue to operate in a peak state. If you do not take time to rest, rejuvenate, focus on your family, and do something outside of real estate, I guarantee at some point you will burn out, lose interest, start making mistakes, and get sick.

I hear time and time again from agents that they *like* to be on call over holiday weekends because they think they are going to get a step ahead of the slacker agents enjoying some much needed time off with their families. I used to be the same way, until I realized that the random showings and appointments I took rarely resulted in a closing - much less a referral relationship of any kind.

Therefore, my first piece of advice is this: mark off every national holiday on your calendar as a free day for the rest of your life. Don't just mark off the holiday, mark off the weekend that surrounds it. Start with the Big Six national holidays. Christmas Day, New Year's Day, Memorial Day, 4th of July, Labor Day, and Thanksgiving.

Take this time. Plan for this time. Your clients are taking this time off, and more importantly, they are going to understand if you are. Customers who do not understand can go find another agent.

The 'All in' Season

Spring and summer without a doubt, is the prime season for real estate. Your referral based business will produce significant steady income throughout the year, but spring and summer is when you have the opportunity to grow your business and harvest additional financial rewards.

It is easy to see why. Not only does your past client activity heat up with the change in the weather, but so do your incoming referrals. Client and customer activity both increase in the spring. It happens every year.

Here in Ohio, I tell my sellers that they want to get their house on the market right around Valentine's Day. That way, when the very first new buyers of the year start to dust off their Realtor.com apps, their property is ready and waiting. If the winter has been particularly harsh, that first glimpse of warmer weather leads to a dramatic increase in activity in March.

Spring and summer is when we have to be in our business and committed 100%. Spring and summer is when I know I will be working late at least a couple of nights a week and probably at least one day each weekend. The business is there. Our clients need our help and this is what we signed up for. It's time to go to work!

The latter half of February, March and April are prime time but there are breaks in the business where things naturally slow down a bit. Significantly, there is a pause in activity during Easter and spring break season. Your clients are taking a break and I want you to take a break here too.

May, June and July are generally the busiest months of the year. We are going to be putting in the time, we are going to be busy, we are going to be having a great time making things happen, and we are going to make a lot of money. But there are natural breaks I want you to take here too.

Memorial Day weekend comes the same time every year and I want you to enjoy it. June tends to slow down every year for a few days around graduation party season and Father's Day. If you can swing it, it's a great time to schedule a weekend or two off. July is super important but again, take the 4th of July off. Independence week is one of the most popular weeks for summer vacations for your clients, so it is a great time for you to take off too.

July is transitional. A lot of business will occur in a short time between the 4th and the last week of the month. By the end of July however, things start to slow down as people squeeze in their last bit of vacation time before school starts again.

Which brings us to August.

August—The Mid-Year Recovery

There is still business to be had in August, but in reality it is one of the slowest months of the year for placing houses under contract and securing new business. It is however, one of the biggest months for closings and your customer service and contract management skills are going to be on full display.

You have just spent six months making the most of your business and opportunity. Whether you want to admit it or not, you need (and deserve) a break. This is the month to take a vacation and back off a few days. Celebrate. It has been a hell of a year so far.

The 'On the Business' Season

While you will still be enjoying a steady stream of re-ferrals over the next few months, the fact is it's time look at the past spring and summer with a critical eye. What worked, what did not, what goals did you meet, and where did you fall short? While September will be relatively busy, and October is a little bit like August with quite a few closings, now through November needs to be where you start thinking about next year's *All In* season.

During the fall, I like to focus on developing new capa-bilities, marketing ideas, advertising plans and financial goals for the next twelve months. I like to make sure I create space to reflect on, and make plans to improve, my business. The pace this time of year is less frenzied than spring and summer. This is the time of year the National Association of Realtors schedules their convention. This is the time of year to get better, sharpen the saw, and set new business goals and standards.

The Holidays

The holiday season in the USA starts with Halloween and spills like a hangover into the first week of January. It happens this way every year. *From a working by referral perspective the holidays are the most important time of the year.* This is the time when making calls, writing notes and cards, giving gifts, going to parties and visiting with your database are the most natural things in the world.

Those agents that approach the holiday season with a plan and sense of purpose can make contact with everyone in their database at least once – and sometimes more than once. During November and December, the seeds you plant, and the referrals you earn, create the closings in January and February that other agents can only dream about. This is an All In season but in a different way than spring and summer.

The Year-End Recovery

Once again, you have done great work the last three or four months and it is time celebrate. Take time for yourself and your family and get ready for the New Year. Christmas through New Year's should be a guilt-free opportunity to enjoy yourself and your accomplishments. After all, spring and summer are right around the corner.

OUR RELATIONSHIP WITH BUFFINI AND COMPANY

OUR TRAINING AND DEVELOPMENT COMMITMENT

Aside from technology and tools, agents express time and time again in survey after survey, that they want more training from their broker. Training at ROOST Real Estate Company is a core value that we never waiver on. Our training and development partners are a company out of San Diego, California called Buffini and Company.

I was introduced to Buffini and Company in 2005. I discovered a world-class group of people who shared my view of the business and helped me become more intentional about my daily business activities. We offer Peak Performer training at least three times a year to our agents, we use Buffini and Company content for our monthly personalized item of value mailings, and we provide Referral Maker contact relationship manager to our agents.

I have personally worked with a Buffini and Company coach at different times in my career, and my results each time far exceeded my expectations. Today we have several agents who have a Buffini and Company personal coach. Each of our offices has a Buffini and Company certified trainer on staff.

We urge you to learn more about why Real Estate Brands Ltd has chosen to work with Buffini and Company at www.BuffiniandCompany.com.

YOUR PAY
YOUR WAY

YOUR PAY YOUR WAY

Whether you are new to the business, an experienced professional, or a team leader looking for the best possible brokerage to build your business with, ROOST Real Estate Co. has a compensation plan and fee structure that grows with you as your business grows.

Your Pay Your Way™ is designed to be transparent, easy to understand, and most of all flexible. It is designed to support both the goals of the agent, the brokerage, and the ROOST Real Estate Co. mission and brand values.

We want to be the first and last brokerage our agents work with.

ROOST Real Estate Co. is a full service brokerage that strives to offer the highest level of service possible, to both buyers and sellers. We are a relationship-focused business, eager to create clients and referral sources for life.

Anytime an agent puts themselves through the emotional upheaval of changing brokerages, they are taking a leap of faith that their new broker has their best interests and goals at heart.

Over the course of a career an agent is going to pay their brokerage tens of thousands of dollars in the form of expenses, fees, and splits. Personal, emotional, and financial commitments of this magnitude deserve the very the best the broker owner and ROOST Real Estate Co. can offer.

We at ROOST™ are always looking for ways to express our gratitude and appreciation to our agents for choosing us.

Ours is a relationship with our agents. We are not interested in a simple series of transactions.

What are the actual costs of doing business at ROOST?

The first commitment a broker has, is the ROOST Monthly Franchise and Marketing Fee. This money is used by ROOST Real Estate Co. to continue to expand the brand through social and other electronic media, upgrade our print materials, and to keep the brand fresh and forward thinking. This fee is equal to 5% of sales and is payable monthly by the broker to ROOST Real Estate Co.

This fee is capped through year 2020 at 5% of gross agent sales or a maximum of $5,000 per agent per year. And, unlike national franchises, ROOST does not collect transaction fees or annual dues of *any* kind.

The second commitment the Broker has, is the Shared Office Expense. This fee is collected to cover the overhead of the physical office space including, rent or mortgage payments, office equipment, phone services, and all of the things required to maintain a business. This fee is equal to 5% of sales and is retained by the broker.

This fee is also capped through 2020 at 5% of sales per agent per year to a maximum of $5000.

The third commitment the Broker has, is to the Administrative Staff including the Agent Business Manager(s) or ABM's. Whether an office has 50 agents or 5 agents, administrative functions have to be completed by someone, and even if this is done in the early days by the broker himself, there is a cost involved. This fee is equal to 5% of sales and is retained by the broker.

This fee is also capped through 2020 at 5% of sales per agent per year to a maximum of $5,000.

The fourth commitment the Broker has, is to the Basic Agent Service and Technology Package. We want our agents focused on working with buyers and sellers. We do not want our agents doing basic marketing and promotion, setting up showings, or filling out contracts with pen and paper. The Basic Service and Technology Package is a commitment from your broker to provide the following:

- Ongoing support for agent training and development. Our brokers are Buffini and Company Certified trainers for Peak Performers – quite simply the finest working-by-referral training program in the world.

- Up to 100 personalized monthly items of value to the very best referral sources in your data base.

- Buffini and Company Referral Maker CRM – The best contact management software in the real estate industry.

- If an agent elects to pursue personal coaching with Buffini and Company – which includes Referral Maker - the brokerage will help pay for the training, up to the cost of Referral Maker as a stand-alone product.

- Dotloop paperless office -- Create contracts and get them signed from anywhere there is an internet connection. Save time and better serve your clients.

- Presentation Brochures – Branded items to reinforce your place with your clients and customers.

- Centralized Showing Service – Never have to stop what you are doing to set up a showing again. CSS also allows you to share feedback from cooperating agents electronically.

- Enhanced Listing Information and personal branding on Realtor.com. Realtor.com is the number one place customers go for listing information. Your personal information will be readily available to all who view your listings. Just as importantly, Realtor.com will send regular emails to your sellers about internet traffic and engagement specific to their listing.

- Dedicated personal cloud based telephone integrated with the corporate phone system.

The actual cost of these services to the brokerage runs from $400 to as much as $600 per month per agent depending on location. There is also a tremendous amount of time involved in working with agents to get the full benefit of the Basic Agent Services and Technology Package.

This fee is also capped at $5,000 a year or 5% of sales through 2020. In our experience agents who take advantage of these services see an immediate increase in productivity of 15 to 20%.

The Fifth Commitment is to the Broker/Owner Herself – The Broker Service Fee. Every fee we have defined so far exists to cover the cost of owning and operating a brokerage. Every entrepreneur expects a return on their investment of time and capital. ROOST broker owners are no different. This is where the Broker Service Fee comes in.

As you will note above, the monthly Franchise and Marketing Fee, Shared Office expense, Administrative Staff fee, and Basic Agent Services and Technology Package add up to 20% of every commission dollar earned by an agent. *However, the most an agent will ever pay in any calendar year for these fees is $20,000 regardless of how much they earn*. These fees are capped to cover actual costs and no more.*

The Broker Service fee is equal to 10% of every commission dollar earned by every agent. There is no cap on this fee. Whether an agent earns $100,000 or $1,000,000 over the course of the year, the brokerage will retain 10%. We structure our fees this way to ensure the broker owners are rewarded and motivated to support elite producers, regardless of their volume.

Our Financial Goals for All of our Agents

We want to see every one of our agents earn at least $100,000 in commissions each year. If that agent is paid on a 70/30 split, they are paid $70,000 and the brokerage retains $30,000.

What if this agent has a great year and hits their $100,000 sales goal at the end of September and still has several closing in the last quarter of the year? Once the brokerage gets to $30,000 the agent keeps 90% of every dollar they earned, for the rest of the year.

For the New Agent

For a new agent just starting out, we offer full service, training, and support with a 60/40 split. Sixty percent of every dollar the agent earns is paid to the agent, and 40%

is retained by the brokerage. The agent is responsible for their monthly MLS(s) fees and a monthly Errors and Omissions Insurance fee of $20 per month.

The 'Power' Agent

Agents with a proven track record earning in excess of $150,000 per year, may negotiate up to a 90/10 split with the monthly Franchise and Marketing Fee, Shared Office expense, Administrative Staff fee, and Basic Agent and Technology Services Package covered with an additional monthly payment. The agent is responsible for their monthly MLS(s) fees and a monthly Errors and Omissions Insurance fee of $20 per month.

The Team Leader

ROOST Real Estate Co. is also the best place for teams to set up shop. Ten percent of commission dollars earned by team members are retained by the brokerage. The Team Leader pays a negotiated monthly fee for the Franchise and Marketing Fee, Shared Office expense, Administrative, and Basic Agent Service and Technology Package fees to the broker/owner. The Team Leader is responsible for their monthly MLS(s) fees and a monthly Errors and Omissions Insurance fee of $20 per month.

Getting Started

ROOST provides every agent with their first 12 yard signs, 1000 business cards, and a www.ROOSTRealEstateCo.com landing page. When you are ready – we will be too. Give us a shout. Your future awaits.

THE REFER YOUR BROKER OPPORTUNITY

Do you think you and your office would benefit from the culture, attitude, environment and opportunity that a Real Estate Brands Ltd affiliation provides?

Why not think about referring your broker/owner to us? We are always on the lookout for Great Fit brokers, owners and managers to join us.

If you think we can help your broker owner and team create a bigger and better future - we want to talk.

GIVE US A SHOUT.

You have nothing to lose and the good life to gain.

A FINAL WORD

WHY SHOULD YOU CAREER WITH US?

Real Estate Brands Ltd. is the place for agents who commit every day to making the real estate dreams of their clients come true.

Real Estate Brands Ltd. is the place for brokers, owners, and managers dedicated to supporting and adding value to the lives and businesses of our agents every day.

Real Estate Brands Ltd. is the place for the buyers, sellers, tenants, and investors that reward us with their business and allow us to help more and more people get where they want to be.

Real Estate Brands Ltd. is made up of the very best real estate professionals in the business building relationships, adding value, delivering results and earning the referrals that allow us to do it over and over again.

ABOUT THE AUTHOR

Chris McAllister is the founder and president of Real Estate Brands Ltd. Chris's unique ability is creating business opportunities and strategies that support and add value to the lives of real estate professionals and their clients.

For more information about our company or our Refer Your Broker program please contact Chris at:

Chris@ROOSTRealEstateCo.com / 844.806.6577

www.ROOSTRealEstateCo.com

www.facebook.com/ROOSTRealEstateCo

www.ingramcontent.com/pod-product-compliance
Lightning Source LLC
Chambersburg PA
CBHW040834180526
45159CB00001B/190